How to Make a Birdhouse

Step-by-Step Instructions and Expert Tips for
Creating the Perfect Nesting Space for Your
Feathered Friends

Table of Contents

Chapter 1

Introduction

Hello DIYer! We're pleased to join you on your journey to building and crafting more delightful creations. This book will give you a step-by-step guide to building a birdhouse for your backyard.

A Brief History

A birdhouse or bird box is a man-made box for birds to live in. It helps give the birds a safe place to rest and live. One of the purposes of these birdhouses is to assist the birds in caring for their young and maintaining their population.

A British conservationist, Charles Waterton, was the first to invent the birdhouse in the early 19th century.

In the mid-20th century, increasing industrialization, urban growth, modern construction methods, deforestation, and other human activities caused a severe decline in the bird population. Birdhouses are getting popular today because not only can they help prevent the decrease in the bird population, people, both young and old, are fascinated by the variety of birds they attract to their homes. Also, the birdhouses themselves can increase the value of your real estate because of the beauty they and the birds bring.

The first birdhouses consisted of pottery made from clay, woven baskets, and other light materials. In the pre-ottoman period, around 1299 to 1922, in what is now known as Turkey, birdhouses were built for sparrows and swallows and made of wood, stone, mortar, bricks, and tiles. They were built into the façade of a building and complemented the architecture surrounding it.

When English immigrants arrived in the Native Americas in the 18th century, birch bark was the primary material used to build birdhouses. The purposes of these structures were not only to increase the number of birds in the area but also to shelter the birds from harsh weather.

We often think of birdhouses as a way to encourage the presence of birds and increase the number of birds in our area; however, that was only sometimes the case. Birdhouses in Europe were initially used as a trap to catch birds and their eggs. These birdhouses were built like a vase made of clay. Early Europeans who came to North America were interested in attracting birds for pest control, and bird bottles measuring about 8.5 inches long and having a small entrance hole of 4 inches were turned horizontally and mounted on the side of buildings. These birdhouses were found in an inventory list from 1746 and were advertised in a 1752 paper.

Whatever the variety in birdhouse use, they have been used to protect wild birds from harsh weather and predators and provide a location to live in most cases.

Importance of Building a Birdhouse

Birds are essential to our environment. They help with pollination and pest control. However, the nests that these handy helpers create are not enough to keep their population from extinction. As stewards of all other animal species on earth, we must care for these birds to ensure they thrive and perform their functions.

Building a birdhouse is one way to help the birds. It keeps them safe and warm and provides them with a space to breed. Birdhouses are easy to create and maintain and require minimal costs and space.

Why Birdhouses Are Important to our Environment

Environmental factors, like the increasing human population, pollution, high-rise buildings, and fewer trees, have made it harder for birds to survive. Birds have their natural habitat taken away by natural calamities and global warming. Birdhouses give these birds an alternative to their disappearing natural habitat. By building birdhouses, we help them ensure the growth of their population and the continuation of their existence. Wild birds prefer the comfort of their nests, however.

The chirping sounds that birds make and the different and beautiful colors of birds themselves are a beauty that can positively affect your day. Bird watching and observing the different types of birds that spark your interest is an inexpensive hobby you can develop when your birdhouse welcomes new occupants each season. All of this gives beauty to your already relaxing backyard.

Building birdhouses as a hobby can also increase your mental and physical activity and keep you active.

Most birdhouses are built a few feet above the ground. This gives the birds a short flying path, encouraging them to fly back and forth from the bottom to the birdhouse. Birds fertilize the soil through the etching effect of their claws while walking on the ground. This makes the soil loose, allowing nutrients to mix with the topsoil. Bird dung creates good fertilizer too.

Flowers also benefit from birds in a process known as ornithophily. This is a phenomenon where birds such as sunbirds, honey-eaters, and hummingbirds pollinate flowering plants. Having a birdhouse means more birds are available to help pollinate fruit trees and other flowering plants. This helps leave your garden looking beautiful and contributes more greenery to the environment.

Some plants depend on birds or insects to carry their seeds to new locations. Birds are among the helpers in that process. When birds eat seeds, the outer coat of the seeds is weakened by their digestive system. These seeds are pooped out through the bird's droppings after they have been digested and are often dropped in various locations, allowing the plants to grow in new areas.

Birdhouses help eradicate pest infestation as some birds eat insects. Insectivores, including bluebirds, cardinals, chickadees, and nuthatches, feed on worms, mosquitoes, beetles, caterpillars, larvae, ants, flies, aphids, grasshoppers, and other pests. Birds feed on these insects to provide adequate nutrition to stay healthy and control their presence in your backyard.

Finally, whether you are planning to sell your property or not, many potential buyers often enjoy seeing birds flutter around the backyard. Birds and birdhouses create a relaxing environment for people looking for a peaceful place to call home and help increase the property value of your home.

Understanding the Basics of Birdhouses

Birdhouses are an easy way to lure birds around your home into your back or front yard. In this guide, we explain how to build birdhouses for different kinds of birds and provide suggestions for setting them up.

Birdhouses come in different types, colors, and shapes. Some designs are simple and plain, while others are colorful with various designs. Some birds are drawn to bright colors, and others are attracted to natural colors to help them blend in with nature and protect them from predators.

Below is a pattern for a birdhouse and a list of measurements you can choose from so you can adapt the design to different species of birds. Customizing the birdhouse you want to build to the needs of the specific bird that you want to have will increase your chances of success.

General guidelines:

1. Wood is the best material to use, and the best type to use is Cedarwood. You can build a birdhouse with at least $2 worth of wood.

   It would be best if you avoided pressure-treated lumber because when it gets wet, it can give off vapors that are poisonous to birds.

2. Preservatives, such as paint or stain, can be used outside the box, especially the back, but not on the inside. You should avoid using creosote as a preservative; The toxic chemical these products produce can harm the birds.

3. Do not use tin cans, milk cartons, or metal for nest boxes. They can overheat and kill the birds that are inside.

4. Drill at least four 1/4-inch drain holes in the bottom of every house to allow rainwater to drain out. Water from rainfall can cause the birdhouse to become damp. Allowing water to drain naturally by gravity will provide a dry space where the birds can thrive and live.

5. Birds need protection from heat and ventilation. Drill two one-inch ventilation holes near the top of each side of the birdhouse to allow enough air to circulate the birdhouse during summer.

6. Providing a hinged side or roof allows you to clean the birdhouse easily. Use rust-proof hinges to make it easier to clean. Keep in mind that other animals can open your birdhouse too.

7. Provide a roof with at least a two-inch overhang on the front portion of the birdhouse to protect the entrance hole from the rain and to prevent other animals from reaching in from above.

8. Only starlings and house sparrows like perches, so avoid putting them if you do not intend for these birds to live in your birdhouse.

9. Keep entrance holes on songbird houses 2 inches or smaller if you don't want starlings and house sparrows to live in your birdhouse.

10. Space boxes at least 20 to 25 feet apart to reduce conflicts because most birds are territorial.

11. Lower the floor 1/4-inch up from the bottom to further prevent rotting. The sides of the house should enclose the floor to keep rain from seeping into the house and nest.

12. Squirrels, snakes, mice, bees, and wasps may enter your birdhouse. If unwanted, carefully remove them.

13. There is no prohibition in State law from removing house sparrows and starlings. So, if you need to remove their nests, you will not be breaking any rules.

14. Birdhouses should not be placed on trees to keep birds from the reach of cats and raccoons.

Suggested Dimensions

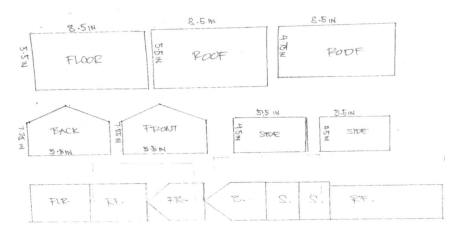

Chapter 2

Different types of Birdhouses

There are many kinds of birdhouses based on the style or material used in building them or the type of bird they're meant to house. Most of these materials are super affordable and may even be lying around your environment. Below are common ones you may have already come across.

Simple Birdhouse

A simple Birdhouse has a classical design to it. It is usually made from cedar wood and mounted on a pole or hung in the yard. This kind of birdhouse takes the shape of a regular human house with a two-sided roof, four sides, and a floor. This kind usually has a hole in the front used as the entrance for the birds.

Fence Birdhouse

A Fence Picket Birdhouse is a birdhouse made from a picket fence or one that is mounted on a picket fence. Like the simple, classical birdhouse, this kind is usually made from wood with an entrance in the front for birds, a roof for their protection, and a platform where they can sit or stand.

Modern Birdhouse

Modern Birdhouses, nowadays, are different from the simple birdhouses that you usually see. Unconventionally, they are typically made of old empty plastic bottles, cardboard, or used containers.

License Plate Birdhouse

As the name suggests, license plate birdhouses are made from license plates, usually metal. They are generally not recommended because the heat will be trapped inside the structure, which is not conducive for birds.

Songbird Birdhouse

Songbird Birdhouses are painted colorfully on the outside to attract songbirds like bluebirds, robins, chickadees, wrens, and purple martins. The colors silver and green should be preferred because they attract songbirds all year round.

Sparrow Birdhouse

Sparrow Birdhouses are houses built to house sparrows and usually have ample room for them to move freely, as sparrows live in numbers.

Peanut Butter Birdhouse

Peanut butter birdhouses are usually made from old or recyclable peanut butter containers. These containers are typically made from hard plastic and are round. These would be more suitable for smaller birds but may not be conducive to the heat.

Gourd Birdhouse

A Gourd birdhouse is a birdhouse made from a gourd. A gourd is the fruit of a vigorous flowering annual vine that climbs on garden structures easily with its tendrils. Many common vegetables like squash and melons are considered gourds.

Log Birdhouse

A Log birdhouse is a birdhouse made from the log of a tree. Its naturally thick, real wood will help insulate birds on cold and warm days and mimic their natural habitat.

Cardboard Birdhouse

Cardboard birdhouses are made of cardboard material, usually of the paper kind. They quickly get wet by the rain and are easily destroyed. Hence, they are typically temporary to accommodate the immediate needs of birds.

Chapter 3

Materials Required to Build a Birdhouse

Cedarwood is the best-recommended material to build a birdhouse. In this chapter, you'll find what other tools you need to make your birdhouse.

You will need the following:

- Wood:

Suggested wood: Cedar picket fence plank

Tools

- Handsaw

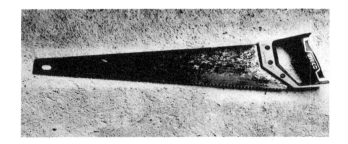

- Hand-powered drill and drill bits

- Forstner bit

- Hammer

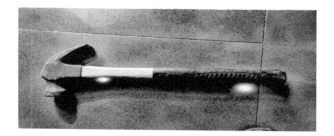

- Clamp

- 1¼-inch nails

- tape measure

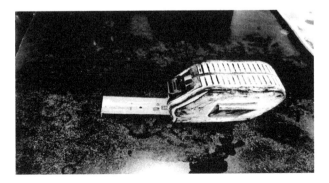

- T-square to make a right angle and 45-degree angles

Chapter 4

Predator Guards

A predator guard is a device that is installed on or below the birdhouse to keep predators away from the vulnerable eggs, nestlings, and incubating females inside the birdhouse.

The nest survival data suggest a 6.7% increase in nest success for nesting attempts in boxes with guards versus those without. This percentage increase may not be the 100% protection that many people believe they're providing, but 7% is a significant increase at the national level. A homeowner can take a few other actions that can improve nest success to a larger extent.

Design Ideas for Predator Guards

The different types or designs of predator guards are:

Cone Baffle Guard

A cone baffle guard is a cone-shaped device usually made from plastic or other materials that can easily be curved and take the shape of an ice cream cone. It is usually placed on top or at the bottom of a mounted birdhouse attached to a pole to prevent other animals from crawling into the birdhouse.

Stovepipe Baffle Guard

A stovepipe baffle guard usually uses duct piping made from metal or steel and is attached to the pole of the birdhouse to protect it from unwanted predators and prevent animals like squirrels from climbing up.

Entrance Extender Guard

An entrance hole extender guard is a sewer-shaped guard that acts like a tunnel attached to the entrance of a birdhouse. It is usually made up of plastic pipe which is 1 to 2 inches wide in radius to narrow the port of entry of the birdhouse.

Noel Guard

A Noel guard is usually made up of a wire mesh attached to a birdhouse's entrance hole. It is generally attached to keep predators from accessing the birds living inside.

Although all types of guards were related to an improvement in nesting success, birds nesting in boxes with cone-type baffles, stovepipe baffles, or entrance hole extenders are more successful. The Noel guard is less successful. Furthermore, birds nesting in boxes with multiple predator guards, like a combination of a cone baffle and a hole extender, were more successful, on average, than birds nesting in boxes using only one type of guard.

Chapter 5

Suitable Birdhouse Mounting Height

Birdhouses should be mounted at least five (5) feet above the ground, if not higher. The surrounding environment around the birdhouse should determine what kind of birds will live in it. Birdhouses that are near the water are more likely to attract tree swallows, while house wrens will use those in gardens.

Wrens and chickadees enjoy birdhouses at a standard elevation of five feet, while bluebirds prefer six feet–purple martins like a height of 10 to 12 feet above the ground. Adequate elevation ensures birds and their nests are protected from most predators on the ground. However, there is no need to exceed a height of 12 feet when mounting birdhouses.

Chapter 6

Importance of Placement

In order to ensure nesting birds are safe, happy, and comfortable, you must carefully select the correct birdhouse location, orientation, and placement.

Which direction should a birdhouse face? East is the most effective placement. Birdhouses facing East get early morning light. Avoid facing birdhouses North because the North winds can threaten the safety and comfort of the birds living inside your birdhouse.

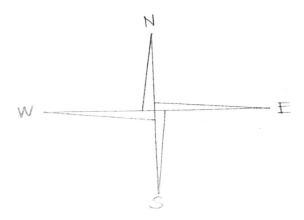

A birdhouse and its entrance hole should face away from prevailing winds. In the United States, it's common for a birdhouse to face East, away from the prevailing wind and the intense afternoon sun.

Chapter 7

Procedure to Build a Birdhouse

Follow these step-by-step instructions with ample pictures to build your birdhouse.

Step 1: Gather and prepare all the tools and materials.

Step 2: Measure and cut the sides.

The illustration plan below shows seven (7) sides you have to measure and cut.

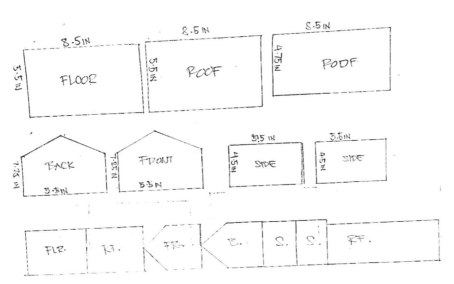

A. Measure and cut the two sides 5.5 by 4.5 inches.

Measure the first side. Using a measuring tape, a pencil, and a triangle square, measure the two sides of the birdhouse at 4.5 inches wide and 5.5 inches tall. Make sure you start on the squared-off end of the cedar plank.

Mark the line where you intend to cut.

i. Marking the first side: Make a mark using a measuring tape and a pencil by measuring 4.5 inches from the end of the bottom of the plank. Mark the wood with a pencil. Draw a straight line using a ruler, T-square, or triangle.

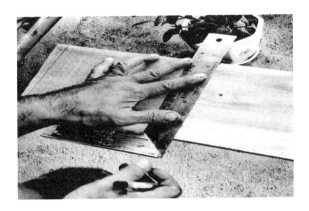

If you don't have a square, you can measure 4.5 inches on each side of the wood and then connect each side with a straight line. Cut the first side of the wood using a saw.

After measuring and marking the first side, clamp the wood to the table to stabilize the wood. Cut the first side off from the wood plank using any saw.

Tip: You want to clamp the cut mark fairly close to the edge of the table. If you clamp it far from the edge, the wood will vibrate because it is unstable. So, clamp it near the mark, so there is no room to move.

If you are going to use a circular saw or a jigsaw, which has a reference edge, line up where you want the cut to be, and then you can hold a speed square or clamp it down to keep the wood still while cutting.

Ride the edge of the saw against the square. This will guarantee a nice straight cut. When using power tools, always use ear protection and eye protection.

It's all right if the cut is not quite up next to the line. The actual height of the side does not matter. What is more important is that the other side is the same height. That is why rather than measuring each side and cutting it out, I prefer to measure one side, cut the first side out, and line it up at the bottom.

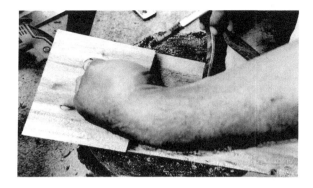

ii. Marking the second side: Measure, mark, and cut the second side. Using a pencil, make a mark or a straight line using the first side as a guide so that the second side can be the same size as the first. Check to see if both sides are the same size.

B. Measure and cut the roof and floor

The next pieces of wood that you have to cut out are three (3) pieces, each 8.5 inches long. These pieces will make up the two sides of the roof and the bottom of the house.

i. Measure 5.5 by 8.5 inches using a measuring tape and a triangle square.

ii. Cut out the two pieces in the same way we cut the 1st and 2nd sides, by measuring using a square, marking the line with a pencil, then cutting using a saw.

iii. Measure the roof's second side, 4.75 inches by 8.5 inches, and cut.

iv. Cut the floor or bottom measuring 5.5 inches by 8.5 inches.

C. Measure and cut the front and the back.

i. Measure the birdhouse's front and back by marking it using a measuring tape, pencil, and a straight edge.

ii. Measure 7¼ inches on one side and 5.5 inches on the other side, and connect each point with a straight line to the middle part of the wood plank, around the 3-inch mark.

iii. Cut to the line. The front side and back sides of the birdhouse should be the same size.

D. Drilling a hole in the front side of the birdhouse.

Now that all of our pieces are cut out, measure and mark the circle for the entrance hole of the bird on the front side of the house.

i. Measure the hole by using a measuring tape and pencil to identify the center point about 3 inches in radius.

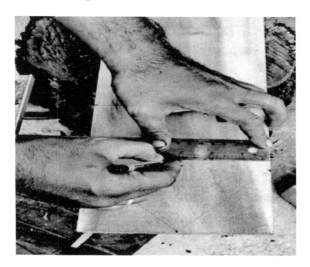

ii. Make a mark to locate the center of the hole that you intend to drill. This should be around 3 inches from all sides of the front.

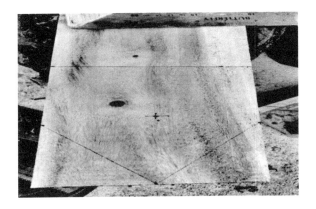

iii. Use scrap wood underneath the front side so that when the drill goes to the bottom side, the drill will go to the scrap wood and not destroy your table. It also prevents the wood from chipping in and out of the circle.

iv. Cut the hole using a drill measuring 3 inches wide. You can make the hole wider or smaller, depending on the kind of birds you intend to live in this house. However, you want to make the hole narrow enough to prevent predators from getting in.

v. Drill from the side of the house pointing inward to get a smoother front-facing entrance to your birdhouse.

vi. Try to get a clean, smooth circle facing the outside of the birdhouse.

vii. Drill the hole, as illustrated in the photo below. If you do not have a drill bit, you can use a saw to drill the hole in the front of the birdhouse.

E. Assemble

i. Gather the tools needed for the assembly of the birdhouse. You will need a hammer and some nails. Next, assemble the cut pieces.

ii. Assemble the two sides of the roof, ensuring that the smaller piece is pressed firmly against the longer piece.

Combine the roof pieces in a side-to-side position. This means that one side of the roof will be longer than the other because of the thickness of the wood. That is why one side of the roof is shorter than the other.

iii. Put about three nails on the roof to put it together. Start hammering the nails halfway to the longer piece of wood before hammering the nails all the way into the shorter piece.

iv. Assemble the two sides of the birdhouse. Attach the first side to the back of the house, as illustrated in the photo below. To align the back with the sides, ensure the bottom is flush with the floor piece because the whole thing will be sitting on the floor of the house.

v. Assemble and nail the second side to the back of the birdhouse.

vi. Nail the other side to the back side, as illustrated in the photo below.

vii. Attach the front of the house to the body.

viii. Attach the floor to the body of the birdhouse. Before attaching, align the back of the bottom of the house, so it is easy to mount. Then, attach it to a wall, or leave it free to sit somewhere. Having the bottom stick out in front gives the birds a space to stand.

ix. Attach all sides of the body of the birdhouse to the floor or bottom of the birdhouse.

x. Nail the floor of the birdhouse to the body.

xi. Attach the roof. Make sure that the back of the roof is flush with the back of the house if you plan to mount it up against a wall; otherwise, you can place the body at the center of the roof.

xii. Nail the roof to the body of the birdhouse. For the nails for the front part of the house, first, align them to the front part before nailing in.

Congratulations!! Your birdhouse is now completed. You have prevented a bird from being homeless and can now enjoy the benefits of having one. You should feel good about what you've accomplished!

Finally, you may choose to mount your birdhouse on a pole or attach it to a wall, depending on your preference.

Chapter 8

Understanding the Housing Needs of Birds

1. Safety and Security

   Birds need to be safe from predators that may attack their eggs or young. Mounting your birdhouse on a pole, away from trees where snakes can easily climb, is preferable. Please, do not hang your birdhouse from a tree. Also, using predator guards to deter squirrels and mice is advisable.

2. Durability

   A property-mounted birdhouse provides stability to the birds that live inside them. Using durable materials like cedar wood to build is the best way to provide a long-lasting and strong house for your birds.

3. Ventilation

   Providing enough space for the birds to flourish and reproduce is a goal that you want to achieve. Using non-metal materials like cedar wood will prevent your birdhouse from overheating in the summertime and suffocating the birds.

Chapter 9

Building Birdhouses for Different Birds

Different birds have been observed to prefer different types of birdhouses. Bluebirds, for example, were observed to prefer a birdhouse with a large roof and a small entrance. When building a house for bluebirds, putting a cone-shaped predator baffle guard is essential to scare predators away. Monitoring their activity is also crucial because bluebirds are becoming scarce. Putting a second entrance hole beside the first entrance hole is recommended to allow bluebirds to defend themselves from the overtaking sparrows, which tend to be smaller than them.

Blue Jays, Mourning Doves, Robins, Barn Swallows, and Phoebes, on the other hand, do not need birdhouses. They tend to nest in shelves or ledges. You can build a platform floor with a little border around the platform with a back piece to be used as an attaching side. Place this platform in areas that are out of your way. You can mount it on a wall or in a safe space, like under the eaves or above a well-lighted place. This platform should be strategically placed 5 to 25 feet above the ground.

Wrens, Tree Swallows, House Sparrows, and Black-capped Chickadees prefer large entrance holes. Make sure you drill an entrance hole that is at least 2 inches in diameter. These birdhouses may be attached to a tree, building, or pole, 5 to 10 feet above the ground. They should be placed 100 feet off cover, like an area with a woody environment. Wrens are famous for taking over the nest areas of other birds because they tend to be territorial. They have been observed to destroy the eggs of other birds that nest near their comfort zones.

Black-capped Chickadees like a well-covered birdhouse. They enjoy having wood shavings on the floor of their birdhouses. They like the entrance of the birdhouse to face away from the strong North winds, so place it facing East.

Purple Martins are observed to nest in colonies, so a multi-level birdhouse is suggested. These structures can be placed 60 feet away from other structures like trees and buildings.

Chapter 10

Monitoring and Cleaning Birdhouses

Cleaning birdhouses is important for the health and safety of the birds and the owners. Dirty birdhouses can attract rodents, insects, feather mites, fungi, and bacteria, spreading diseases to birds and their young. Cleaning your birdhouse will avoid health dangers. A clean birdhouse increases durability and enables the structure last longer.

Clean your birdhouse after the first hatching of the eggs and when the birds have flown away. Cleaning once in a breeding season is enough. In warm areas where birds hatch their young more than once, birdhouses can be cleaned in between each time a new family settles to encourage more nesting. Tap gently on the roof to check if your birdhouse is occupied. If the birds are still present, wait another week before checking again to give the birds plenty of time to vacate the home.

How to Clean a Birdhouse

1. Open or detach the roof of the birdhouse. Birdhouses with swinging sides, hinged roofs, or removable fronts are the easiest to clean.

2. Remove all old nesting materials and scrape out any feces or clumped matter. Please dispose of the fecal matter in a plastic bag or bury them in a compost pit to create healthy fertilizer for neighboring plants.

3. Scrub the house thoroughly with soap and water. Bleach may be used to eliminate bacteria. Thoroughly scrub all corners and creases.

4. Rinse the birdhouse well with water to remove all traces of soap or bleach.

5. Pat dry to avoid dampness.

6. Inspect the house for loose hinges, protruding nails or screws, prominent splinters, and other hazards that can injure adult or hatchling birds.

7. Repair any damage to your birdhouse to keep it safe.

8. Check to ensure that all ventilation and drainage holes are not clogged. If needed, drill additional holes to provide extra ventilation or drainage to improve the house.

9. Reassemble the house securely and ensure all screws, hinges, and joints are tight. If the house converts to a winter bird roost box, assemble it in that configuration after the breeding season ends so birds can use it for safe shelter.

10. Store delicate gourds or clay birdhouses for winter to last longer, or return wooden birdhouses to their hooks or posts to be used as roost boxes for cold winter nights.

Chapter 11

Typical Problems Encountered
In Building a Birdhouse

When your birdhouse is empty, it could become frustrating and seem like the birds are just avoiding you. However, that may not be the case.

First, observe and learn which kind of birds uses your birdhouse. You may need to add feeders, water features, and comfortable shade to attract them.

Early nesting birds may explore your birdhouse for additional broods later in the season. Putting your birdhouse up early in the season can help attract early nesters. Have your birdhouse ready in late winter, so it's available for nesting birds.

Some birds can be very picky in their choice of birdhouses. Building the right kind of birdhouse specially designed for the type of bird you want will go a long way. Also, you should learn more about the kind of bird that you would like to attract and then build or adapt your birdhouse to their specific needs and likes. You can refer to chapter 9 on Building Birdhouses for Different Birds to learn more.

When your birdhouse is not mounted at the correct height, it could pose a challenge. Where you mount a birdhouse is just as important as the size and shape of the house itself. Some birds will use higher houses, while others prefer houses closer to the ground. Understanding birds' preferences can help you position birdhouses properly. Chapter 5 of this book explains the different heights that birds nest in and their preferences regarding whether the house is mounted on a pole or tree or if it is hung. Chapter 6 of this book is a very helpful guide on how to place your birdhouse properly.

The entrance/ hole of your birdhouse can become worn out and bigger than what you want it to be. This problem can be easily solved by using the right dimensions and the proper entrance hole size suited to the birds you want to attract. You can also repair the already worn-out ones. Adding an extra cover plate over the existing hole is the easiest way to fix a birdhouse entrance. The plate should be made of solid material that will resist chewing, gnawing, or scratches, such as thick plastic.

Center the new hole in the plate and double-check that the new entrance is the proper dimension for the birds that use the house. Smooth the rough edges around the hole's rim so it will not attract young birds to chew on it or injure birds as they move in and out. The plate can be glued, nailed, or screwed in place. You can also add a thick extender to create a small tunnel leading into the birdhouse to fix an enlarged entrance hole. Furthermore, you can replace the entire front panel of the house when an entrance hole has been severely damaged.

You may want to recycle your birdhouse; however, birds that used to nest in them will often only reuse your birdhouse once. Some birds may reuse some of the nesting material to build a fresh nest. One way to encourage the reuse of the birdhouse is to clean it out after every brood has fled so the house is clean. Cleaning out the birdhouse also reduces the risk of dangerous contamination or infestation from old feces, feather mites, or other insects. Unused birdhouses may be recycled for roosters or other smaller pets like hamsters.

Bigger animals like snakes, squirrels, and mice can threaten birdhouses. Like other animals, birds want a safe place to raise their young. Adding safety features, such as predator guards or baffles, as shown in chapter 4 of this book, will help protect brooding birds. Perches should be removed, and the house design should include drainage and ventilation for safety and comfort. Keep your dogs and cats indoors and take the necessary steps to deter feral cats and other unwelcome predators from your yard.

Larger, unwanted birds may seek refuge in your birdhouse. An inappropriately large entrance hole can entice larger birds, such as house sparrows or European starlings, discouraging the smaller birds you want to welcome. These larger birds may even kill hatchlings or brooding adults. Placing a suitably sized and smaller entrance hole will keep out unwanted birds while letting in smaller and more desirable birds. Observe the right kind of birds you want to attract and adjust your birdhouse to a height that the birds can easily access and eventually nest in them. Chapter 5 of this book explains the different heights you may want to place and mount your birdhouse to solve this challenge.

You may want to take a photo of the birds inside or around your birdhouse, but nesting birds should not be disturbed by flash photography, frequent peeks, or other intrusions that can stress brooding adults and young chicks. It is better to take a photo from a distance and focus your device to get a closer angle.

https://www.thespruce.com/top-bird-house-problems-386677

Chapter 12

Troubleshooting: Birdhouse Building Problems

Problem No. 1: Injuries

Before working on your birdhouse, avoid injury and accidents by wearing proper protective equipment like a pair of workman goggles, construction earplugs, and construction gloves.

Problem No. 2: Instability while cutting the wood

In cutting the first side marked in step 1, clamp the wood to the table to stabilize it during cutting. You want to clamp the cut mark fairly close to the edge of the table, so it doesn't have room to move. If you clamp it far from the edge, the wood will vibrate because it is unstable. If the cut is not quite up next to the line, that is all right, as the actual height of the side does not matter. What is more important is that the other side is the same height.

Problem 3: Uneven sides

When cutting the second side for the birdhouse, you want to be careful so that both sides are the same size. Rather than measuring each side and cutting them out, measure one side, cut that side out, then line both sides up at the bottom before cutting the second side.

In cutting the bigger side of the roof, use the bigger side of the roof as a guide to mark the floor side so that both sides can be the same size.

In cutting the second and smaller side of the roof, use the thickness of the first and larger side as a guide to mark the portion where you will cut out.

In cutting the front side of your birdhouse, use the back side as a guide to mark your second side so that both the back and the front side are precisely of the same size.

Problem 4: Damage to work table

When drilling a hole in the front side of your birdhouse, as illustrated in step 5, you should use scrap wood underneath the front side so that when the drill goes to the bottom, it will not destroy your table.

Drill from the outside of the house, pointing inward so that you expose your birds to the smoother side. The outer portion will tend to be rough as the wood tends to chip away and expose pointy tiny wood chips. You do not want the birds getting hurt by these exposed wood chips.

Problem No. 5: Instability in assembly

In assembling both sides of the roof, as in step 6, hammer the three nails halfway into the longer side before hammering the nails all the way into the shorter side of the roof. This will allow you to move your roof to the proper position and give you room for adjustments because, in this step, the wood pieces tend to move and become unstable while hammering the nails.

Problem No. 6: Difficulty mounting the birdhouse

To properly mount your birdhouse to a wall, align the backside of the bottom of the house to the wall before attaching it with nails so that it is easy to mount or attach your birdhouse to the wall. Give the birds standing space by extending the floor of the house unto the front. If you plan to mount it up against a wall, make sure that the back of the roof is flush with the back portion of the house. This will allow you to mount it properly on a wall or fence.

Problem No. 7: Nail doesn't get to the front

In nailing the roof of the house to the front side of the body of the birdhouse, align the nails first and make sure that the pointy side of the nails will hit the front side of your birdhouse mid-thickness as the nails are hammered through.

Chapter 13

Tips and Tricks for Building a Birdhouse

https://www.bobvila.com/articles/make-a-birdhouse/

Tip No. 1: Build birdhouses according to bird specificity. Build a birdhouse for a nesting bird that lives in the habitat where you plan to put in a birdhouse.

Tip No. 2: Build the right size house and hole dimensions. Different species of birds require different-sized houses and entrance holes. Inside dimensions must be large enough to accommodate the incubating bird and a brood of growing young. Entrance hole size is especially important. If the hole is too small, the bird you built the box for won't be able to get inside. If the hole is too big, predatory birds and animals can get inside and reach the nest, and cavity-nesting birds may not use the house.

Tip No. 3: Use the proper materials. Wood is the best material for building birdhouses. Other materials (like metal or plastic) may not insulate the nest enough, so eggs or young could become chilled in cold weather or overheated in warm, sunny weather. When building, you can use rough-cut wood slabs, tree sections, or 3/4-inch plywood for best results. Never use creosote-treated wood, as creosote may kill eggs or chicks.

Tip No. 4: Use galvanized nails, as these will not rust. Birdhouses need not be painted, but the box may last longer if you paint the outside. Never paint the inside of a birdhouse. If you paint the exterior, use dull (not bright or glossy) colors that blend in with the surroundings. Nest boxes that don't match the vegetation may be easier for predators to find.

Tip No. 5: Build a birdhouse that will stay dry and warm. Place the roof of the birdhouse at a slight angle and extend it over the sides and front of the box. This way, the roof will shed rain or snow and protect the entrance hole and sides from dripping water.

Tip No. 6: Drill four 1/4-inch holes in the floor to provide drainage if water seeps in. The sides of a nest box should extend down beyond the floor so that water won't leak in.

Tip No. 7: Provide adequate ventilation. Drill small holes (1/8 to 1/4-inch diameter) through each side of the birdhouse just below the roof to provide better air circulation.

Tip No. 8: Do NOT add perches. Perches allow predatory birds (like jays, magpies, ravens, and crows) better access to the eggs and young in a nest box. In contrast, cavity-nesting birds rarely use perches and prefer houses without perches.

Tip No. 9: Be sure young birds will be able to leave the nest. Roughen the inside of the nest box below the entrance hole or attach a sheet of 1/4-inch galvanized wire mesh so fledging young can climb out easily.

Tip No. 10: Provide woodpeckers, waterfowl, and owls with nesting material. Many cavity-nesting birds will add their own nest material, but woodpeckers, waterfowl, and owls prefer nest boxes with 2-3 inches of dry sawdust or woodchips at the bottom.

Tip No. 11: Place the box carefully. Put your birdhouse on a sturdy pole, post, tree, or under a house eave. Freely swinging birdhouses are rarely used. Be sure to place the birdhouse at the proper height and in the right habitat for the bird you want to attract (see distribution and habitat information in the dimension table). Face the entrance away from prevailing winds.

Tip No. 12: Don't overcrowd an area with nest boxes. Most cavity-nesting birds defend territories, so don't overcrowd an area with nest boxes for a single species. Usually, nest boxes should be placed 50 feet or more apart. Swallows, however, will tolerate neighbors and sometimes nest in "apartment" birdhouses.

Tip No. 13: Build your nest box so that it is easily maintained. Construct the birdhouse with a roof or floor that can be easily removed so you can reach inside to clean it.

Tip No. 14. Maintain your nest boxes. Nest boxes should be cleaned out each spring and disinfected to prevent the spread of avian diseases. Be sure to dry the inside and (if necessary) add fresh, dry sawdust or woodchips.

Tip No 15: Materials should be at least ¾ to 1 inch thick. Wood should be used to insulate the nest during colder and warmer months. Be sure to add a few ¼-inch drainage holes in the floor to keep the interior dry.

Tip No. 16: Ensure the roof is angled and has ample overhang to keep the rain out.

Tip No. 17: Avoid using metal for birdhouses. Birds need proper ventilation; metal or materials made from steel will produce heat that may suffocate the birds inside, especially during summer.

Tip No. 18: Use a hinge to attach one side of the roof to make it easier to clean your birdhouse.

Tip No. 19: Even if the birds do not care how your birdhouse looks on the outside, they care about how your birdhouse can provide comfort and safety on the inside. Having this in mind, please keep your birdhouse simple.

Tip No 20: Do not use treated lumber, as the chemicals can be harmful to the birds. You may opt to use a light stain or sealant instead of paint. If you choose to paint your birdhouse to make it colorful and attractive to some bird species, paint only the outside to prevent exposing the birds to the harmful chemicals that paint contains.

Tip No 21: Use durable materials that can withstand the weather and be recycled for the next season or other uses. Cedar or redwood is affordable, comes in 1" x 6" sizes at your local hardware store, and will last for years outdoors. Exterior-grade plywood is also another preferred choice. Instead of using nails, try to use screws and wood glue to make your birdhouse more durable.

Tip 22: Ensure your birdhouses are as clean and safe as possible for nesting or roosting backyard birds. Clean the post or hook where the birdhouse is positioned to remove any lingering pests or bacteria from the area. Clean your birdhouse properly, and provide a safe, happy home for your birds.

Chapter 14

Conclusion

Building a birdhouse is simple if you follow the step-by-step guide that this book provides. It can be done with under $3 worth of materials, depending on where you live, and you can use whatever basic tools you probably already have in your home.

You should give yourself a pat on the back after building your birdhouse because you've contributed to preserving the ecosystem and provided a safe home for birds to repopulate.

Now that you've built one, you can go ahead and show it off to your friends and neighbors and let them know how they can make theirs as well! However, more important than showing off is knowing that the animals around us are happy, safe, and can function as they were created. Remember, we must care for this earth and the things that are in it, and it starts with the little things.

If you've enjoyed reading this book, subscribe* to my mailing list to get exclusive content and sneak peeks at my future books.

Check the link below:

http://eepurl.com/dCTyG1

OR

Use the QR Code:

(*Must be 13 years or older to subscribe)

Made in the USA
Middletown, DE
29 September 2023